A Memory and a Wish...
Poems of Life.

Erin Lyn McGraw

iUniverse, Inc.
New York   Bloomington

A Memory and a Wish
Poems of Life

iUniverse books may be ordered through booksellers or by contacting:

iUniverse
1663 Liberty Drive
Bloomington, IN 47403
www.iuniverse.com
1-800-Authors (1-800-288-4677)

ISBN: 978-0-595-52445-7 (pbk)
ISBN: 978-0-595-51176-1 (cloth)
ISBN: 978-0-595-62499-7 (ebk)

Printed in the United States of America

THIS BOOK IS DEDICATED to all those people who have been in my life at one time or another. Whether it was for one day, six months or twenty years, you made a difference to me, somehow. Some of you are gone now, leaving me with lessons learned and some continue to teach me and be with me through it all. Without any of you, there would be no poems to write. So, I thank every single one of you.

I would also like to thank my family and friends who continue to support me as I pursue my passion for writing. I could not do this without your support. Thank you and I love you all.

Introduction:

This book of poems and memoirs is a testament of life. It takes you down the journey of life's ups and downs and everyone's search for love and dreams coming true. It is about opening your heart to give and receive love, even if you end up with a broken heart. Lessons that we need to learn in this lifetime, some make us stronger, and some can knock us down for a while. Life is so fragile that we need to take every day and make it the best. Touch other people's lives that are not as fortunate as we are, for we never know when we will need others to reach out to us. Life is filled with the sorrow of saying good-bye to people that we care about and love. Whether it is through death or other situations, people come and go out of our lives. But the ones we love that have gone to a better place continue to watch over us in love. Some things in life we just don't understand, the way the world has changed, how someone can hurt someone else so deeply, without a reason. People that walk around with so much hurt and anger in their hearts, not knowing which way to go. All we can do...is be the best person we know how to, love all we can, and live our life with no regrets.

So…. go out and make lots of memories with those you love, and make lots of wishes and believe that anything is possible and they can all come true. Just sit back, have faith and watch as your dreams come true.

This poem is about a high school friend who battled cancer for two years and unfortunately lost his fight three months before I graduated from high school. Growing up in a small mountain town, things like this didn't happen, especially to someone just seventeen years old. And for a close group of friends that were living life carefree and immortal, just being teenagers, it was difficult to understand it all. It is difficult to understand death as an adult but you never think you are going to have to deal with it as a teenager. But we made it through, because we had each other and our special friendship. A special bond that will always remain between us. A bond that no one can ever take away or truly understand. It made us closer friends and made us appreciate each other and life more. It made us realize that we were not immortal. Our friend taught us about strength and courage. The way he dealt with his illness, treatments, and impending death was truly inspiring, even today. I feel privileged to have called him a friend. And he will never be forgotten. He will remain in our hearts and memories forever. May he rest in peace.

(More about his story is told in my book, "The Journey of the Terminally Ill-Through the Eyes and Heart of a Hospice Nurse". Available at amazon.com, barnesandnoble.com and iuniverse)

Roads

It has been such a long hard road
A road filled with uncertainty and fear
A road you traveled with such courage and strength
Now the road has finally ended,
Along with all the pain
And suffering.

This road was rough and painful
Traveled only by you,
Everyone else just followed
Never knowing exactly what you were going through
But we continued to be right behind you, holding you up
And even when you pushed us away
We continued to see you through in spirit,
Knowing we would all meet again at the end.

The end of this road is filled with sadness
For it hurt us to see you suffer
And it hurts us because you are gone,
But there is a certain kind of peace,
Because even though we don't know where you have gone
Or what it is like there,
We know that you are no longer suffering
And you are at peace.

We all stood there at the end of this road
Knowing you were no longer physically with us
So we silently stood to say our good-byes,
Stood and stared,
Wondering,
Why you were taken from us.

All of us wiped our tears
Knowing that we could not stay there forever,
So we all turned around and headed back
Back down the road of life
Walking hand in hand
Knowing we must continue on,
Without you,

Even though our lives took different roads
And your road was shorter then ours,
We each have lessons to learn.

But there will always be a comfort in knowing
That you are watching over us
Protecting us,
And guiding us
As we continue down the road of life.

***Dedicated to a friend who lost his battle with cancer my senior
year of high school, you have not been forgotten***

I wrote this poem my senior year of high school and it was read at the graduation ceremony. Looking back, when you were in high school, you thought that was "the world". Everything was so important at the time and everything was such a drama. Everything bad that happened to you, you never thought you would live through it, but you did. It is so difficult to realize that there is a whole big world out there with endless possibilities and lessons to be learned. Everyone was so scared on graduation day, scared to be going out into the "real world". Leaving the sheltered little town most of us had called home our entire lives. A lot of us had known each other since kindergarten and the thought of them not coming with us was terrifying, because they had always been there. We were already feeling lost without them. But on graduation day, there was a moment where we all just sat there together and soaked up all the memories of the past twelve years. Not knowing what lie ahead for any of us.

Now as an adult, high school is a distant memory, and so are most of the people I sat with that day at graduation. Although it is an accomplishment to graduate from high school, I have realized that high school is such a small part of your life. A small part of who you are. Half the time you walked around feeling so confused about who you were and where you belonged, always trying to be someone else. It was a time of rebelling, experimenting, confusing heartaches, broken friendships, confusing lessons, and weird changes to your body. There is so much more out there and the lessons learned after high school are important life lessons. You will fall down several times out there in the "real world", but get back up and learn from your mistakes, be a better, stronger person because of them. Never let anyone tell you that you can't do something or be somebody, take that and help it make you stronger and more determined, prove them wrong. You can do whatever you want and be whatever you want. Never give up on your dreams, so dream big, do what you love, follow your heart and your passion and you will end up right where you are supposed to be.

Finally

We made it
It is finally our time to shine
And tonight as we sit together in our graduation caps and gowns
We will shine together
One last time.

Everyone has been through good times
And bad times here,
But we always had each other to celebrate with
Or lean on for support,
There was always a shoulder to cry on
Or a hug waiting for us just around the corner,
For these memories will never be forgotten
Because they are so special.

Now it is time to prove ourselves
As individuals,
To break away from the safety we have known for so many years
Something that never let us fall,
But now we need to find out who we really are
And exactly what we want for ourselves.

But right now as we sit here
 Let us remember all the memories
And take time to laugh a little,
Cry a little,
But be happy for ourselves and each other
Because we finally made it
It is finally our time to shine,
One last time.

Everyone has a natural fear of never finding that someone special to spend the rest of their life with. This poem is from the female perspective of that fear. Wondering if he is really out there, is there really such a person for me? What happens if there isn't or if we never meet? Then I will never get to experience all the things I wish to experience with someone I love and someone who loves me back with the same intensity. Of course, every little girl, and even grown-up girls, dream of their wedding day, and having the fear that they will never have that day come true. That you will never have that one special day where you can live in your own fairy tale, whatever that is to you. And when you are out there in the "dating world" it is easy to get discouraged about never finding the right match for you. Endless blind dates gone wrong. Pulling your hair out and screaming, wanting it all to end. Wondering how much longer you have to go through this. And the fear of wondering how much worse a first date can get. Asking the question, why me? What have I done for love to be so difficult to find?

Will I Ever?

Will I ever meet the man of my dreams?
The man whose kiss I feel all the way to my toes
And who's touch leaves me breathless
Every time he touches me.

Will I ever have that moment when you know that you will be
together forever?
The moment where you look down and see a shiny ring on your
finger
And as you say "yes",
As he whispers in your ear how much he loves you
And then holds you tight.

Will I ever have that day?
My day,
The day I have dreamed of since I was a little girl
Where I get to wear my mother's wedding dress
And walk down the aisle with my parents by my side
With the love of my life waiting for me at the end.

Will I ever have that one special moment?
Where it is just my dad and I dancing to a lifetime of memories
That have gone by too fast
But still feeling like his little girl in his arms.

Will I ever get that special "first" dance with my husband?
The touching song and dance
Which brings everyone to tears
As all our friends and family look on,
So happy we finally found one another.

Will I ever have the chance to love someone with my whole heart
forever?
To make them happy
And be there to support them during the tough times
To take care of one another as we age
And be together until death takes one of us away.

Will I ever have the chance to be half the mother my mom was?
To experience having a life grow inside of me
And watching them grow,
Teaching them about life
And love,
Letting them know that they are so loved
And I will always be there for them
For they will be my world,
Will I ever?

This poem is about the flood of feelings and emotions when you first meet someone. The sparks are flying; your heart is beating out of your chest, sweaty palms, butterflies in your stomach, and the fear of saying or doing something wrong. You want to know everything about that person and you want to know it now. You secretly want to be the one they choose to spend the rest of their life with. But you know it is too soon. It is about wanting to know what is inside a person, their pain from the past, what has hurt them so you don't hurt them again. It is about knowing how to comfort but yet giving them space. Getting to know what makes them love and trying to be that special person in their eyes. Every time you are with them your mind is going a million different directions, with a flood of emotions. Feeling so impatient, wanting to know what they are thinking, where is this going, and is it you? And in the back of your mind you are wondering what they are thinking about you.

I Want to Know

I want to know what makes you smile
What lights you up inside
What inspires you
And makes you glad to be alive?

I want to share those moments of happiness with you
The moments of laughing until you cry
And your sides ache,
The moments where you can't stop smiling even though your cheeks
hurt.

I want to know what scares you
And why,
Your deepest fear
And your scariest moment,
And what got you through it all?

I want to bring you comfort in times of fear
Letting you know that you are not alone
For I will be right beside you
Being scared with you,
But still seeing you through it all.

I want to know what makes you angry
What makes things worse
And what can calm you down,
What are things that you can forget
And what are the things that you cannot forgive?

I want to be the one that will calm you down
Or just simply listen
Not saying a word,
The one that will simply leave you alone if that is what it takes
The one that is not afraid of apologizing for something I did to make
you angry
And will never be the one to do something that you cannot forgive.

I want to know what makes you cry
What touches your heart,

Hurts your feelings,
Have you ever had a broken heart
And has it ever healed?

I want to be the one that dries your tears
The one you sit and talk with about everything
Knowing that I will always be there to listen
Or hold you,
All the while, wishing I could take all your pain away
I want to be the one that will never break your heart
But only fill it with love and trust.

I want to know what makes you love
What leaves you breathless
Makes your heart skip a beat,
What do you find beautiful
And what passion lies inside of you?

I want to be someone you can love
Someone who leaves you breathless
Always wanting more,
I want to release the passion inside of you
And make your heart skip a beat,
I want to help you be all that you were meant to be.

I want you to feel safe with me
For I will never lie
Or betray you,
Will never leave you
Or stop loving you.

I want to know what you think of when you look at me?

Everyone has a mother; unfortunately, I know that not everyone is lucky enough to have a loving mother whom is always there for you when you need her. Some people have mother's that have just gotten up and left. Others have mothers that are emotionally unavailable, struggling with addiction problems, and their own personal demons. I, however, am very lucky and am thankful everyday for the mother that I have. And my heartaches for all those that don't have it so lucky and will never know what it feels like to have a loving, available mom. And all those who have mothers that abuse them or have abused them in someway in their lifetime, I wish I could take your pain away. For no one deserves to experience that kind of pain or fear from someone who is supposed to love you.

This poem is dedicated to my mother and for everything she did for my siblings and I. It is also for all those mothers around the world that sacrifice everyday and love their children with their whole heart. Respect your mother, for she gave you life, and that in itself is an amazing thing. I hear it is the hardest job in the world. Learn from your mother, for she has lived. Be thankful for everyday you have her in your life, and appreciate everything she has done for you.

I just hope that someday I can be to my children, half the mother my mom was to me.

I love you mom, thanks for everything!

Mother

You took my little hand with your finger and helped me walk
When I fell
You were right there to pick me up
And taught me to keep getting up after each fall,
To never give up.

You were so patient with me
While I learned to tie my shoes
Spell my name,
And no matter how many times you had to correct my grammar
You remained calm and loving
You helped me learn,
Never giving up on me.

There was a comfort in knowing you were the last person I saw before
school
And knowing that you were always home
Just in case I would need you,
You would be there
And you were always there to pick me up after school and take me
home.

You were the one that tirelessly stayed up all night
When I was sick or scared
You were never very far away,
And that is something I will never forget
That comfort and love meant more to me then you will ever know.

As I try and find out who I am
And what I want,
You are still beside me
Telling me of your experiences
And mistakes,
Allowing me to experience my own.

Even though I am grown now
I will never stop needing you
And sometimes when I don't feel good
Or get hurt,
You are the first person I want with me
Because nothing helps more then just having your mom with you,
So please always stay close
Because you never know when I will need you again.

I will never be able to give back what you have given me
Or thank you enough for everything you have done
To help me be the person I am today,
I just hope that one day,
If I could just be half the mom that you were
To my own children,
That will be a start.

Sometimes in life, when you least expect it, someone amazingly wonderful appears in front of you and changes your life forever. They are everything that you have dreamt up in your head and now they are standing right in front of you. Time stands still when you are with them and you can talk for hours without any awkward moments of silence. It is like you have known each other for a lifetime and are just picking up where you left off. To have that feeling in your heart that everything is finally as it should be. And that someone finally thinks and feels the same way you do. You truly get each other from a soul level. To have someone in your life in which you just seem to fit together perfectly, and naturally. Never wanting to be away from them but liking the excitement and anticipation of seeing them again. Feeling arms around you in which you feel you could live inside forever. To have an unforeseen connection between two people in which you both know when one is thinking of the other, and you can actually feel that energy inside of you. It is truly amazing what love and strong emotions are capable of.

Melt

When you gently brush my hair away from my face
And place it behind my ear,
Tender kisses on the neck
Simple short glances when our eyes meet,
These are the things that make me melt.

Hearing your voice on the phone
Being held so tightly in your arms
Feeling so safe, protected
And cared for,
These are the things that make me melt.

How you say or do something just to get me to smile
Hearing your laugh,
Seeing your smile,
And looking into each other's eyes that are saying a thousand things
Without us even saying a word,
These are things that make me melt.

The concerned look on your face when you know I am hurting
The gentle brush of your hand on mine
When you tell me I am beautiful,
And the ever so gentle kisses when your lips touch mine,
These are the things that make me melt.

Cuddling up next to you just talking and laughing
Having you lye next to me at night
Knowing I get to wake up with you beside me in the morning
Having our legs crossed over one another's,
These are the things that make me melt.

Thinking of you when we are apart
The anticipation of seeing you again
Having your arms around me once more
The feeling of my heart beating faster when I am with you,
These are the things that make me melt.

When you take care of me when I am sick or hurt
Just knowing you care enough to be there
Even though you can't do anything,
The comfort your presence brings to my soul is enough,
These are the things that make me melt.

When you hug me from behind
When we hold hands and neither one of us ever wants to let go,
Hoping the time with you never has to end
Wanting to be next to you in anyway I can,
These are the things that make me melt.

These are the things that make me wish there was some way I could
just melt into you
And stay there forever.

This is a poem about a very special hospice patient I took care of a few years ago. She was kind enough to open up her life as a terminally ill patient and became an inspiration and a dear friend. She opened my eyes to life. She taught me that it is possible to keep your spirits up in any situation, even when you are dying. She also taught me that you truly can find humor in anything if you choose to. She would always say, "Laugh a lot, life is funny!" It made me realize that we need to spend more time loving, going out and having fun, and less time worrying and being scared. There is always room in your life for caring and laughter. Take chances and gain the wisdom from knowing that you took the chance even if things didn't work out the way you wanted them to. She also told me to, "Live with no regrets, and do not fear death." She was truly one of the most amazing people I have ever met. I miss her a lot sometimes but know that she is watching over me, making sure that I don't spend my life worrying over everything. I hope everyone has a chance to meet someone as incredible as her, I know I feel very thankful that I did. And if you don't, please learn from what she taught me.

(Her entire story is told in my book-"The Journey of the Terminally Ill-Through the Eyes and Heart of a Hospice Nurse"). Available at barnesandnoble.com and amazon.com

Don't Cry

Don't cry for me
For I am ok
And I am exactly where I am supposed to be
In the arms of my love once again.

It was time for me to leave my diseased body behind
It was starting to smother who I was
And it had served its purpose
I did everything I was sent here to do,
It was time for my soul to travel on
I have so much to do on the other side.

Don't be afraid
There is never any reason to be afraid
And if you ever find yourself feeling scared
Draw courage and strength from my guidance
And remember you are never alone.

Do not mourn the loss of me
But celebrate my life
For it was filled with laughter and love
Remember me with a smile,
Not tears.

Know that I will be celebrating my freedom
Freedom from sickness and pain
I am at peace now,
And I wish for you to be at peace with me.

Do not cry for me
For I am not really gone
I will watch over you
So be good,
And continue to talk to me
Because I will be listening,
And continue to laugh
And know that I will be laughing with you.

In times of loneliness, uncertainty
And pain,
Just think of me
I will be the one wiping away your tears
Giving you the strength to make it through
And spreading my angel wings around you,
To hold you tight in comfort and in love.

Do not cry for me
There is no need for tears
Or sadness
For death is not the end,
But it is the beginning of a beautiful new adventure.

***In memory of my very special patient, my forever angel, that
touched my heart forever and taught me about life and living.***

Some of us have been very lucky to find that one special someone that captures our heart and holds onto it forever. And even when this person steps out of your life for a while, when they come back you still have the same feelings for them. And when you see them there, there is a sense of relief in your heart, relief that you are home. And you always feel the same intensity in your heart, which tells you that they are really truly special. And even when they go away, that feeling stays with you. I can't really fully understand how after thirty years of meeting someone, they can still have your heart. I guess that is the funny thing about love. I don't think that we are supposed to fully understand it; I think we are just supposed to feel it. And hopefully everyone will be as lucky as I have been to meet that special someone that grabs onto your heart, and whether they are in your life or not, there will always be a special bond between the two of you, no matter what the future holds.

Always Been You

All those year's ago
When we first met
I saw something so special in you
Something you did not yet see in yourself
And even when you hurt me,
I knew you didn't mean to
Because I could see the real you.

Even though we soon parted ways
You were never far from my mind
It is only now that I realize
That I never really let you go,
Because no matter who I was with
I was always wishing it was you,
For it has always been you.

Year's passed without having you in my life
Except for in my dreams
For when you were in my dreams
You were always right by my side
Which made me wake up missing you,
And longing to have you in my life again.

I tried so hard to find you
But every effort failed,
And my heart would sink further every time,
For you were nowhere
Except in my dreams,
Then I finally realized there was nothing else I could do
But wish you well
And hope that you were happy and loved.

Then many year's later
Fate stepped in,
A phone call I had tried to make several times before was successful
And hearing your voice that night took my breath away,
Something inside me finally felt peaceful,

For I knew somehow that I had been given a second chance,
The chance I had only dreamt about was right in front of me
For it has always been you.

Seeing you was like home to me
Being with you made me feel so safe and comfortable
Something I never thought I would feel again,
And all the emotions I had held so deep within me
Came to the surface
Feelings I had only felt with you,
I felt like everything was as it should be
For it has always been you.

I opened my heart to you
A heart that had been shattered so many times
Had life again,
And for once I was not afraid of taking a chance
Or getting hurt,
Because it was with you
For it has always been you.

I knew as soon as I felt your arms around me
That I was finally safe
I took the deepest breath
And let go of a lifetime where I had been hurt,
Afraid,
Let down,
And could no longer trust.

To feel you kiss me again made me want to melt into you
The way your kisses always made me feel
And that is something I did not ever forget,
Or experience with anyone else
For it has always been you.

It is like a dream having you back in my life
But every time I am with you
It is so difficult for me to walk away
For I fear that if I do,
I will turn around to find that you are gone

And I never want to lose you again.

No one knows what the future holds for us
Or the purpose of this second encounter,
But I will cherish every moment with you-
Like the night beneath the tree
And the starry sky,
Just talking and listening to music
It was the most amazing night of my life
A night that I want to live in forever.

I know it can all end tomorrow
Or it might go on for years,
And I will always be hoping that things grow into the amazing
possibilities I have always
    Seen
And felt between us,
But even if we don't end up together
And no matter where our journeys take us
I will always want you in my life.

Because you will always have my true heart
You always have,
For it has always been you,
And it always will be.

The love between a father and daughter is a special thing. Unfortunately, I know that not everyone has been as lucky as me to have a wonderful father in his or her life. Some people don't even know their father, other's are abused by their father or they walk out on them just when they need them the most. To a little girl, your father is someone you look up to, someone who knows everything and protects you. A father has endless advice and endless stories of his childhood. Sometimes we get stubborn and think that we know best but in fact it is he who has lived and knows from experience. Father's should be role models to their daughter's, for it is that type of man she will someday look for to build a life and family with.

I have been very lucky to have such a wonderful father. He is my role model and has given me so much good advice and is always there for his family. And when I was at my lowest, most confusing times in my life he always seemed to know exactly what to say to make me feel better. He has always made me realize that life isn't easy but the hard times don't last and things always get better. And as I sit here writing this, as a grown woman, there will always be part of me that wants to stay his little girl forever. Sitting on his lap listening to bedtime stories, all safe and protected where no one could hurt me.

This is dedicated to my father and all the other wonderful father's out there that go above and beyond for their children and families. Loving them, protecting them, and providing for them. Be thankful for every day you have your father in your life.

I love you dad, thanks for everything!

To My Father

As a little girl you were the one I looked up to
The strong one that could scoop me up in your arms
And carry me to bed
The one who had the answer to every question,
No matter how many questions were asked.

The man who taught me how to ride a bike
Build a tree house,
Played board games after dinner almost every night,
The lap I would sit on for a bedtime story
Never feeling so safe and protected
As I did sitting there with my little head resting
On your chest.

The anticipation of lying in bed at night
Not wanting to go to sleep,
Until after you came in to kiss me good night on the forehead
Letting me know how much I was loved,
And knowing you would be there during the night to protect me,
And would greet me in the morning.

Now that I am grown
Trying to figure out the challenges of life,
You are still the one I come to for questions
And you still seem to have all the answers,
The one who can fix and build anything
And the one that helps me understand,
That life isn't always going to be fair.

You are my role model
The only man who has never let me down
And when my heart gets broken,
All I want is to be that little girl again
Curled up on your lap,
Safe and protected.

Whenever things go wrong
And life seems so confusing
And unfair,

As the tears stream down my face
All I can think of is home,
Because there is no better place to be
Then in the arms of my dad.

Because even though I am grown up
There will always be part of me
That is your little girl,
The little girl that still needs your wisdom
And the love and protection,
 I have always found in your arms.

And when I find that special guy
The one that steals my heart away,
A part of my heart will always belong to you
Because you will always be my dad,
And I will always be your little girl.

Everyone is looking for love and it seems so difficult to find. Sometimes we make bad decisions, stretch things a little bit, just trying to be loved. This poem is kind of like a plea to give love a chance. Give that someone in your life a chance to love you and you might be surprised at what they can offer. Open your heart and let someone in, no matter how difficult it is and how many times your heart has been broken. For it just might be when you are about to throw up your arms and give up that that special someone will be standing right in front of you. It is also about a promise of love. Knowing that love and relationships take work and you are willing to give it your all. Going into love wanting it to last forever and being willing to do whatever it takes to make that happen.

If You Let Me Love You

If you let me love you
I promise to love you with my whole heart,
Your world will be filled with nothing but love
Every tear will be kissed away,
And your heart will never be hurt again
For I will protect it with everything that I have.

If you let me love you
I promise you a lifetime of laughter
For I will always be by your side,
With ears ready to listen
And my arms will always be there to hold you.

If you let me love you
Whatever life brings to us
I promise we will get through it together
Just hold my hand a little tighter,
And we will walk through it together.

If you let me love you
I promise to love you through it all
To never let you down,
I will support your dreams and ideas
And celebrate who you are,
I will love you until I take my last breath
For this is forever for me.

Sometimes in life there are periods of time where nothing seems to be going right. So when you find that special someone that takes you away from it all, you want to hold on to them and never let go. They calm you and make you feel safe in such an unsafe and confusing world. Give you hope on love when before you had none. The world is so much better when they are close to you and in your life. Everything is a little bit brighter, happier, and safer. And with just the touch of the other person they can actually make the rest of the world disappear for just that moment in time. Something that is truly magical and should be treasured! It is when you do finally find that one special someone to build a life with, it is then that the world does finally seem at peace and so does your heart. And that is when you can finally take the deepest breath of your life, because your search is finally over.

World Within a World

In a world of such uncertainty
Pain,
And confusion,
You are the only thing that makes sense to me
You are the calm and grounding
I have been missing all these years.

Just when I thought there was nothing
And I had lost hope in so many things
You showed up,
Back in my life
Giving me hope again,
And a soft place to fall.

I need you in my life
Because every time I am with you
All my troubles
And fears seem to just dissolve into you
I am then finally at peace,
My heart is where it should be.

And just with a touch of your hand
Or gentle kiss of your mouth
You can make the whole world melt away,
Where there remains just the two of us
Which is what I want,
What I need.

You are all I desire
You are my world within a world
Within a world of uncertainty,
Pain,
And confusion.

I would rather live in your world
Which is filled with safety
Love,
And peace.

This poem is written about a hospice patient that I took care of for only a short time but that is all it took for their love to inspire me. They had been married for close to sixty years and every time I made a visit I could still feel and see the love between them. It did not matter that he was in a coma and could not communicate in anyway, because they still had their own little way of communicating with each other. And she always knew what he needed. Watching them was amazing and inspiring to know that that kind of love actually does exist. And it proves that true love between two people does not need words or even eye contact, for it is all in the heart and soul. She took amazing care of him considering she was elderly and not in good health herself. She would talk to him like she always had; she just didn't get any response from him. But she knew he could still hear her and feel her each time she would kiss his forehead. She could feel that he was not going to last long, even though there were no physical signs of this. But in the end she was right, because she knew her love. Even though I only knew them a short time, I can still remember the way she would look at him and talk to him, as he laid there in bed non responsive. I will never forget the love that I could feel between them each time I came to visit.

Lifetime Love

He is all you have ever known
You don't remember life before him
And can't imagine life without him.

He has made you laugh
Made you proud,
Angry,
Even frustrated at times.

But now you realize you wouldn't trade any moment with him
Because as you gently stroke his hair
Kiss his forehead,
And gently whisper into his ear,
You know that he is slipping away
And you will never see his smile,
Or hear his voice again.

After all these years
All of life's experiences
Good and bad
He was always by your side
Your best friend,
Never letting you down.

You have loved him every day you have known him
And even after all these years
Sometimes when you look at him
You wonder if it is possible to love him even more,
You gave him your heart
And you have shared a love so deep
And powerful that it is indescribable.

As you lye next to him
You think back to times when lying next to him
Brought you feelings of such love and security,
Nights where you would spend hours talking
Laughing,
Loving.

As you drift off to sleep in his arms
You always knew he would be right beside you in the morning
He always made you feel so beautiful and loved,
And it is now that you realize he is your lifetime love.

Now lying next to him brings you feelings of sadness and fear,
You are afraid to close your eyes
So night after night,
You force yourself to stay awake
And stare at his chest,
Carefully watching it rise and fall with each breath
And as you hear him breathe,
You wonder which one will be his last.

Wanting to hold on so tight
Thinking of how you can keep him here
Never wanting him to go,
Because he is your life,
Your breath.

But a part of you knows that you must let him go
Because you know that the body next to you is no longer him,
It is time for his suffering to end,
If you only knew how to let go
And had the strength to say good-bye.

The night so peaceful and still
And after several sleepless nights
You finally allow yourself to drift off,
What seemed like seconds
Turned out to be hours,
And you are suddenly startled awake,
Immediately glancing over at him
It is then that your heart stops,
And so does your life.

You know he is gone
But you still put your head on his chest
Just like so many times before,
Only this time you can't listen to his heartbeat

Because there is nothing,
Just the silence of the night.

You are surprised to find that you yourself are silent too
Realizing you don't have the strength to make a sound
There is just a flood of tears,
And the pain you feel in your heart is making it difficult to breath
You suddenly feel guilty,
Thinking that your love was not enough to keep him here.

He knew that you didn't have the strength to let him go
So he was the one who had to decide it was time to go,
And that is when he slowly slipped away
Knowing as much as he loved you,
His love for you couldn't keep him here either,
Nothing could.

Even though he physically had to leave you
He went with peace and love in his heart,
Because he knows that true love never dies
And he will continue to be with you
Right by your side,
Where he has always been,
As your lifetime love.

As a registered nurse I have had the privilege in my nursing career to work a lot with cancer patients and their families. Some of these patients are still getting treatment, still having hope. Others are terminal, getting ready to say good-bye to the ones that they love. And in every one of them I found an incredibly inspiring, courageous, full of life person that I admired greatly. No matter how sick they were, they continued to fight and even if they knew they had lost the fight, they continued to live. Their loved ones that stood by them through it all were also very inspiring, special people. They did not walk away when things got tough, they stood a little closer and continued to give support and encouragement. Even when they got the news that no one wants to ever hear, they continued to hold their head's high and continued to support and care for the one that they loved. They continued to care and support them until the last breath was taken. These people are all heroes to me, every single one of them. I will never forget my experience caring for them and their families and friends. I will not forget their faces and the courageous way that they faced their illness with a smile, faith, and love. And when it was time to face death, they faced that with courage as well, and lived as fully as possible until they were gone. Neither patient, family, nor friend ever gave up on living and life even though life had in some way given up on the them.

Thank-you all for allowing my to be part of your journey, whether it ended with living or with dying. I will never forget any of you because you inspire me on a daily basis. Thank-you for all being such hero's to me, touching my heart and making me realize what life is truly all about, and what it means to live.

Hero's

For those of you who have fought with such courage
Pushing through the difficult days where all you wanted was to give up
And holding your head up when you didn't think you had the
strength to,
But it all paid off
For you have won,
And for that-
You are a hero in my eyes.

For those still fighting with everything that you have
Keeping the hope alive with each breath
Refusing to be beaten by this awful disease,
Even though sometimes you feel it would be easier to just let go
But everyday you get up and you FIGHT
And for that-
You are a hero in my eyes.

In memory of those that kept fighting
Against all odds
They would not give up
Not until the very last breath was taken
Even though they lost the battle,
You are not forgotten
And because you fought so hard,
You will always be remembered as a hero in my eyes.

And for all of you that selflessly loved,
Cared for,
And supported those you loved,
Standing by them through it all
Watching as they lost strength and hope,
And even when your fear was growing
You never faltered,
Never stopped loving them,
No matter what the outcome,
And for all that you did
And so much more-
Every one of you is a hero in my eyes!!

**This poem is dedicated to all of those whose lives have somehow
been touched by cancer, I admire you all!**

This poem is about meeting a childhood friend that I had not seen or had any contact with since elementary school. We, unfortunately, met at a classmate's funeral. I recognized him right away because he looked the same, just all grown up. And as we stood there after the funeral talking and catching up, there was suddenly an extraordinary amount of connection, energy, and attraction between us. Strong enough that I could actually feel it. It is something that neither one of us had ever experienced before and we were both completely surprised by it. Staring into his eyes I saw our souls together, and that is something I could do forever. And when it was time to go and he hugged me good-bye, there was something in his hug that said a thousand words and emotions. There was some force that day that was pulling us together because it was so difficult to leave his side. I felt like that was where I belonged. The energy between us did not fade. It was the start of something so incredibly special that I will never forget it in my whole life. We understood each other; we "got" each other and knew what the other one was thinking by looking into each other's eyes. I don't know if it was love but it was something more powerful then both of us could control. Something I could never have imagined happening. I don't regret one minute we spent together, one word that we spoke, or one hug. But I miss the feeling of being with you.

Home

We were just little kids when we first met
Knowing nothing about life
Except play,
How safe our world was then.

We were only in each other's lives for a short time
But I remember you,
And wondered what happened to you
For you just seemed to disappear.

Now as adults we meet again
And our world is no longer what it once was,
For we have both been through life experiences
Good and bad.

And as our eyes met
They locked and we remembered year's ago
And then something extraordinary happened,
Even on a day filled with sorrow,
For we all gathered to say good-bye to a friend we had lost.

My life was changed forever that day by you
For in the mist of grief,
Sorrow,
And the uncertainty and fragility of life,
That faithful day when you stood before me
All grown up,
I looked into your eyes and saw my soul.

I cannot explain what happened that day
I don't think anyone can,
There was something very powerful between us
Something I felt through my whole body,
From your heart to mine.

And when you held me that day
All the pain and chaos of the day disappeared
It was silent,
Just you and me in our own special place

For I was home.
Your kisses said more then I ever thought a kiss could say
And whenever you looked at me,
Everything just faded away
And I knew I was home again.

You took a heart so broken
Confused,
And afraid,
And somehow finally made it feel something besides pain
Then is when I realized that I forever belonged in your arms.

I don't know why we met that day
But am thankful for ever minute I got to be with you
Because that was a minute in my life where I felt safe
Cared for,
Loved,
And beautiful.

It was place I wanted to stay in
Forever,
For it was that special place
 I have been searching for my whole life
And there it was in your arms,
It was home.

Sometimes it is so difficult and painful to try and understand why people come into our lives and make us love them so much and then leave. The person you count on to be there for you in good times and bad. And even if sometimes you crossed that line and became more then friends, your friendship was always more important. It is the friendship that you miss the most and as you look around and they are nowhere to be found. Left without any explanations, making you stop and wonder if it was something you did or said to make them leave. But deep down you know that it is never you that makes someone leave. They leave because of something they are struggling with within themselves, which makes it not possible for them to be in your life at this time. Sometimes they come back and sometimes they are just gone forever. We all need to hold our friends close while they are with us and make the most of the time we have with them. Because no one knows how long someone is supposed to stay in our lives and we could turn around at any time and they could be gone. So make lots of memories and tell them how special they are to you while you have them. True friendships are very hard to find, and all friendships need to be treasured and we need to be thankful for every one of them. Whether they last two days or twenty years, hold them close as long as you can.

The Friend in You

I miss the friend in you
How when you would smile it would light up a room
And my world,
I would always end up smiling too.

I miss the friend in you
The friend that was always so calm,
Making me believe that everything was going to be alright
No matter how hopeless,
Or lost I felt,
You gave me hope with your inspiring words.

I miss the friend in you
The person that was first on my list to tell good or bad news to,
Because you were such a support to me
Such an important part of my life.

I miss the friend in you
The friend that somewhere down the road,
Stole my heart away
My whole heart,
And then you disappeared.

I miss the friend in you
Everything about you
And even the things I don't know about you,
I miss having you be part of my life,
I miss my friend,
And I want you back.

This is a story of a little girl I met while I was doing some school nursing. I can still see her face clearly in my mind and remember every detail of the horror of abuse she went through. It is difficult to understand why anyone would harm a child, but unfortunately, it happens everyday. It happens way too much. I don't know why it happens to some children and not others, I guess it is just part of their journey here; maybe some kind of lesson they need to learn. It is very difficult to swallow though. All you want to do is hold these children and show them love and tell them that everything is going to be all right. But it is not ever going to be ok, because the emotional scars of abuse stay with them forever, even affecting their lives as adults. Yes, some of the physical signs will fade but that child inside will never be what they would have been if they wouldn't have been abused. They will always have a shattered soul. Their world is not like ours, it is scary, unsafe, and untrustworthy. And a lot of times they are placed back into the same home to face more abuse (whether it be physical, sexual, or emotional), it doesn't matter. Abuse is abuse, in any way, shape or form. Sometimes sadly, their little bodies and souls just can't take anymore so they leave this earth, to go to a peaceful place where there is no pain, and they can be anything they want to be. But that means there has been a life ended at the hands of another. A person that was supposed to protect them, love them, and keep them safe, but they let them down. And the world has also let them down by not speaking out.

Please keep this child's story in mind and if you ever suspect child abuse or abuse against another person, of any kind, please call police. Maybe together we can prevent another shattered soul from being born.

Shattered Soul

Her eyes were so dark you could see your reflection
But deep inside they were void of love
And you could see all the sadness
Fear,
And confusion behind them
Along with a shattered soul,
Too young to understand why.

For someone could not control his or her anger
And took it out on her
Now, because of that,
No one will ever know what she could have been,
For she is now left with a shattered body that didn't work
And a shattered soul,
At the hands of another
Who simply just walked away.

Those she loved let her down
Those who were supposed to protect her from pain and harm,
Will she ever trust again?
How can she ever trust anyone
When the very person who gave her life let this happen
What is left,
Where does she go from here?

No one can begin to imagine the physical pain she went through
How scared and alone she must have felt,
Fear we can't even comprehend as adults
Happened to a precious, innocent child
That had done nothing wrong,
But was let down by this world.

I wonder why her soul did not set her free that day
To a place where she could be free from all pain
And just be,
Will she ever feel the touch of love without being scared,
Will she ever know what it is like to be held in someone's arms
And feel protected,
Without feeling pain

Will her life of pain and fear ever end?

She's too young to understand why her body doesn't work right
Or why she can't talk like the other children,
Play like the other children,
Or why she will never be the complete,
Beautiful, intelligent woman she had the potential to be.

The image of her beautiful little face haunts me at night
Images of her story that I read would put a chill through anyone,
But somehow, she still finds the strength to laugh
And smile,
A smile that would melt your heart.

I find myself wiping tears from my eyes
Wanting so bad to turn back time for her
To take her pain away,
Pain she doesn't understand
And doesn't deserve to have.

Her shattered body will heal with time
But she will never be what she would have been
Her soul will always be shattered,
And every time she closes her eyes
She will never feel safe,
And will always wonder if or when it will happen again.

This is just the story of one child
One face among millions,
That are abused and have been abused in someway during their
lifetime
Abused by those that were supposed to protect them,
And just love them,
But instead they just let them down,
And chose to look the other way,
Not wanting to see.

How does this keep happening?
Whose eyes are not open-
Whose ears do not hear the screams of these children,
The children who do not understand,

The bodies and souls that are now shattered for life,
They are now just a shadow of what they could have been.

Another shattered soul is born into this world.

Dedicated to anyone who has been scarred and changed forever because of some kind of abuse, at the hands of another. I hope someday you can find some kind of peace in your heart. And to all those that we have lost, but their souls set free, because they just couldn't take the pain anymore. Rest in peace.

Most people believe in something, or someone higher then ourselves. And some people don't believe in anything at all, which is ok too. But for me, I do believe that there is something bigger and higher then we are that guides us, protects us, and makes sure that we learn our lessons and reach our destiny. This poem is in reference to a hospice patient I took care of a few years ago. Before she died, she made me a promise that after she died she would find a way for us to continue out relationship, just on another level. To be honest, I was skeptical at first but after she died she would send me signs. The signs were subtle, like the smell of a particular flower, and that is when I really believed. Yes, I talk to her because I know that she is listening. Sometimes she brings me answers right away and other times she makes me wait until I learn my lesson first. Knowing what I know now has brought me a lot of peace because I know that I am not alone. We are not alone, we each have something, or someone watching over us, if we choose to believe. Sometimes it is just a feeling of "knowing" inside that they are with you, and that is when you have a peacefulness come over you. She kept her promise, she was a very determined person in life and I knew if anyone could find a way she could. I am thankful everyday for her guidance and protection and for whoever else is "around" me, protecting me and helping me when I feel lost and alone.

Bear in mind that this is strictly my perspective and based on my experiences. I am not judging anyone for what they believe, or don't believe. And I am not trying to convince anyone to believe what I do; I want everyone to believe whatever brings you peace in your heart. Don't allow others to tell you what to believe or who to believe in. Sometimes I feel that beliefs are pushed upon us and it doesn't "feel" right to us inside, but we go along with it anyway because of society or family pressure. It is you that needs to find your own peacefulness, and develop your own beliefs and not let anyone else tell you differently. Whatever comes to you is ok, as long as it brings you comfort in difficult times, in times of pain, and gives you comfort when you feel alone and scared. Just take some time to be completely silent and listen to your heart and what is inside of you, and follow what feels good and right for you. Don't worry about what others think.

Forever Angel

You are my forever angel
Watching over me when I am scared
Giving me comfort,
And when I am sad
Or not sure I can go on
You are right there,
Holding me up
Giving me strength,
Never leaving my side until you know I can stand on my own again.

You are my forever angel
It is such a comfort knowing
You will be there when I need you,
And when I don't think I need you
You are still around,
Sometimes just because you want to be near me
To make sure that I am having fun
And behaving myself.

You are my forever angel
Sharing the joy's of life with me
The little thing's in life that matter so much
Laughing with me,
Celebrating with me,
Just like you promised you would,
Thank-you for keeping your word.

You are my forever angel
Always there listening to me
Even when I babble on,
Or cry myself to sleep
You are there,
To make sure I reach my destiny.

You are my forever angel
Never letting me down
You are always there when I call on you,
It is when I don't call on you
That I turn out to need you the most,

And you always know somehow
Because you are always there.

You are my forever angel
You bring me peace,
Give me guidance when I feel lost,
You will always be in my heart
And everywhere I need you to be,
I am forever grateful for you
For I would be lost without you.

You are my forever angel
It is hard to believe how long it has been
Since I said good-bye to you on that cold February afternoon
Never forgetting what you told me
And that was that you would find a way to always be with me,
For us to keep in touch with one another
And you have been with me ever since,
Just as you said you would
You truly found a way
Because you are,
And always will be,
My forever angel.

This is a poem that is close to my heart. It is the story of how I met one of my best friends. I was working as a chemotherapy infusion nurse in a clinic. When she walked in I knew right away she was someone special, someone I have to get to know. I felt a connection towards her and knew before we met that we would become friends. She had such a positive attitude about what was happening to her and never once heard her complain and she would always come in with a big smile on her face that would light up the room. As soon as her chemotherapy treatments were done I quit the job because I felt in my heart that the only reason I was there at that particular time was to meet her, so my purpose there was done. It is strange how circumstances and the universe bring people together and make sure they meet. We became fast friends and learned from one another. She taught me about strength and courage and I helped her through one of the most difficult and frightening times in her life. She always tells me that me just "being there" saved her life.

We are still the best of friends and she is now celebrating five years of being cancer free from breast cancer. After a few more bumps in the road after her treatments, she is now healthy. She continues to inspire me to this day with her attitude and strength. She is truly an amazing person to me, one of my personal hero's and I am so thankful that we met. She has changed how I look at life and live my life. We support each other through life's difficult times, celebrate the good times, and always treasure our friendship. We should all live like that. I hope we have many, many years of friendship ahead of us. But we both know, and have experienced, how life can change in a heartbeat and that is why we need to treasure those that we love. Because life's road can be pretty bumpy at times and everyone needs a shoulder to cry on, a kind ear to listen to, and to know that you are loved.

Special Friend

A room filled with so much fear,
Uncertainty,
And sickness,
Each chair filled with a person
A person with a story,
Fighting for their life
And their loved ones trying to keep the hope alive
Standing by them through it all,
With the unspoken word that not everyone will survive.

There in the corner chair
Sat an extraordinary woman
Her smile would light up the room
Her laughter was contagious,
And she always came in with her head held high
Even though she was completely bald
She wore it with pride and grace,
I had never seen such a beautiful face.

I did not know her
Or her story,
But I couldn't help but wonder what she had been through
What she was going through now
And what lie ahead for her,
And those that she loved.
How could this happen to such a beautiful spirit
So full of laughter and life,
She did not belong there.

Her spirit was radiating
Her courage and determination was inspiring,
And I knew that if anyone could get through this
It would be her,
For she had the inner strength to do so,
And she just would not have it any other way.

Every time I poked through her skin with the needle
And watched as each drop of chemotherapy went into her body,

There was an ache in my heart for her,
And I said a little prayer to the angels
To make her better,
To take away her pain,
And give her some peace in her heart.

When the last drop of chemotherapy was through her body
I had the privilege of being there
And there is nowhere else in the world I would have rather been
For she made it,
A day I will never forget
For I knew that my job was done there
It was time for me to move on,
And it ended with an embrace and tears that touched my very soul.

I am so proud to call you one of my closest, dearest, best friends!
You continue to inspire me with your courage
Laughter,
And attitude,
I am a better person for knowing you
 I now know why we were both placed at that clinic at the same time,
And I am forever grateful for that divine intervention.

I'm proud to walk beside you once a year
Among thousand's of others
To celebrate life,
Hope,
And friendship,
Thank-you for allowing me to be part of your journey.

I look forward to a lifetime of friendship with you
With lots of memories
Laughs,
Good health,
And dreams coming true,
For we both deserve nothing but the very best.

I love you and thank-you for all you have taught me
The friendship you have given me,
A friendship that I treasure close to my heart everyday!
Dedicated to my friend, Jan, a breast cancer survivor!

This is about being thankful, and not just around the holidays, but everyday. For some people every day is a struggle, a struggle to stay alive, provide for their families, and deal with the loss of someone that they love. We should consider ourselves the lucky ones to have our friends and family in our lives to love and make memories with. All if this can change in an instant, for life is so fragile. Things don't always make sense and it is sometimes difficult to understand why some have to go through such hard times, but life is not easy. Hopefully, those going through hard times will find some sort of peace and that someday the hard times will end. The pain in their hearts will be a little more bearable.

None of us knows what lies ahead on this journey of life. That is why we should live fully in the moment and love one another as much as we can. Forgive those who have wronged us in some way, because not forgiving only hurts us. Do not take your life or anyone's for granted, because it can be gone in a blink of an eye. Live without regrets.

Make your dreams come true.

Holiday Time

As we gather together during this holiday time
With the ones we love surrounding us,
Instead of bowing our heads,
We need to proudly look up into the faces of those that we love.

We need to be thankful that every chair is filled
With someone we love
And someone who loves us,
For we have been lucky
To have had them in our lives for yet another year.

As we celebrate our loved ones
And life,
Let us not forget those we have loved and lost along the way
Those who continue to watch over us
Even today,
As they will live on in our hearts forever,
Never to be forgotten.

Take a moment to think of those families
That gather around a bed today,
Hoping their loved one will make it through another night
For they are struggling to say their final good-byes,
As they know that each breath,
Could easily be their last.

Think of those families that have loved ones far away
Fighting so we can be free,
Sacrificing the ultimate
For strangers like us,
Giving their lives,
When we have asked nothing of them.

And for those families
Who are sitting around a table like us
Except their table has a empty chair,
Where someone they loved once sat
A life taken in someway,
Leaving them to wonder why,

And how they will ever go on to face another day.

For families who have no table
Or chairs to sit on,
And barely enough food to eat,
Who cuddle together in winter jackets and blankets to keep warm,
Let us keep them in our thoughts
For they have fallen on hard times,
Let us hope that better day's are ahead for them.

On be-half of those not so lucky,
Let us remember to open our hearts to everyone
Be thankful for everyday,
Love fully,
And love everyone
Do not judge, for we do not have the right,
We need to instead live our lives as fully as we can
Everyday,
For we never know when it will be our lives that will be changed
forever.

We have all at one time or another experienced a broken heart. Someone who left us or things just didn't seem to work out. Sometimes its hurts so much you are not sure you can make it through. But sometimes, things just are not meant to be and it is difficult to see it that way when you are hurting. Within time though, when you look back you realize that it was for the best because someone better was out there for you. You can't turn back time and make things right with someone who does not want to be with you, especially when they are already moving on with someone else. So, you need to find the strength within yourself to walk away, no matter how difficult that is, and try and move on. For in life there, unfortunately, will be many other broken hearts before you find the person that will not break your heart. It is very difficult to understand when you feel that you really have found that special someone and they end up breaking your heart. It is ok to cry, grieve, scream, whatever you have to do to feel the pain that they have caused you, and you will feel so much better after you do that. Then it is time to move on, for you can not hang on to the edge forever when they are never going to come and pull you up; tell you they are sorry and everything is going to be ok. Real life does not work that way. You have a choice to let them win by falling into a deep depression, or showing them how strong and wonderful you are and that you don't need them and don't deserve to be treated like that. That is when you will come out a winner, and a stronger person. You will then be available for someone better to come along.

I think love is one of the hardest lessons of life. And I have had heart break after heartbreak. But after each one you learn something about yourself so you don't repeat it again and it does make you a stronger and more independent person.

Letting Go

It has been so hard letting you go
You cross my mind all the time
I miss you,
And every time I hear your voice
Or see you,
There is an ache in my heart
An ache for things to be better between us.

I want so bad just to look into your eyes again
Talk to you,
And to melt into your arms
Where I always felt so safe,
I never wanted to leave.

I miss your tender kisses that took my breath away
Gentle whispers in my ear that made my knees go weak,
And how you always made me smile
Even when I tried not to,
Or didn't think I even could
You could always bring a smile to my face,
Carrying my worries away.

Losing you hurts,
All I can do is take it one day at a time right now
And hope someday the pain will go away,
Because I know I can't change things
I can't bring you back.

Everything that happened with us hurts
And so do the thing's that didn't happen, that we just talked about,
It is so difficult for me to realize
That your arms will no longer be there to hold me
And I have to find the strength to go on,
Without the person I thought would hold me forever.

Everyone who is single out there has an image of what kind of love they want in their life. This is a picture of the love I want. A love that lasts through the good times and the bad. A love that is filled with laughter and love. A love that lasts forever until death takes one person away. But even then, the love will continue to live on because it remains so strong. I know that to some it sounds like a fairy tale and that love and relationships in the "real world" just aren't like that. But I disagree, because I have seen this kind of love caring for the terminally ill patients and their spouses. Love like this does exist, rare but it is out there. And I believe that as singles we should not settle for anything less then our "dream love". Whatever that picture looks like to you, hold on to it, believe in it, because you deserve it. For we are all seeking love, and it is turning out to be a lot more difficult then I ever thought it would be. But I just keep hoping that this means it will be all that more special when it finally does happen. So, don't sell yourself short because love of all kinds is out there and I truly believe that if you don't settle and wait for that one person you were supposed to walk this life with, love will be everything you dream of and more. So just keep that in mind when you are feeling discouraged. It does exist, truly deep from the heart and soul because I have witnessed it and we should settle for nothing less then that.

The One

I want you to be the one to wipe away my tears
To hold me tight through the tough times,
No one else's arms will I feel as safe and protected in.

I want you to be the one that makes me laugh
The one that I can laugh with
And to make you laugh too.

I want to be the one that loves you
With my whole heart
To give you more love then you ever imagined
I want us to love each other,
No matter what life brings us,
I want our love to pull us through
And keep us together.

I want you to be the one I grow old with
Experience life with,
I want to walk beside you for the rest of my days.

I want you to be the one I wake up to
And lye down beside every night,
Knowing the comfort that you will protect me
And be there in the morning.

I want you to be the one that is always there for me
Never letting me down,
Someone I can depend on,
One that will never leave me
Or hurt me.

I want you to be the one in which my heart is safe with
The one who supports my dreams,
Listens to me,
As I will support your dreams
And listen to you.

I want you to be the one holding my hand
As I go to the other side

Knowing that our love is too strong to ever die,
I will continue to be with you in spirit
And we will be together again,
As I will be the one that is there to take you when it is your time.

I want you to be my life
My love,
My heart and soul
For I love you,
And life without you would not be any kind of life at all,
For you would not be in it.

I want you to be the one
Always and forever walking side-by-side.

We have all been affected in one way or another by school violence. Especially the students that lived through that day or lost a friend that day. I can't imagine the horror they must have seen, and probably still do from time to time. I can't remember when it started, but I would give anything to have it back the way it used to be. The day's when school was fun, a place to learn, grow, make friends, and feel safe. I don't understand what has changed that much, where has all this hatred and violence come from? And how can we stop it? School has it's own challenges without worrying whether you are going to make it through the day alive or not. Why does it have to be this way? Let's just all hope that someday it stops, and goes back to the way it used to be, the way it should be!

Dedicated to all those lives out there that have somehow been affected and changed forever by school violence. For those still on the painful road to recovery, I wish you strength to recover and go on. And to all those who have lost someone in the violence, my thoughts are with you and I hope that someday you can find some sort of peace!! And a special thanks to all the hero's, because without them, more lives would be lost!!

Shattered Dreams

So many dreams were shattered starting with a single shot,
Happening over and over again,
School is supposed to be a time of fun
Friends and laughter,
Learning,
Growing up and finding yourself and deciding to be somebody,
It is about dreams coming true.

Dreams that have ended for so many
Now all they know is chaos and horror,
Wondering if there is any place that is safe anymore?
All those that made this world a better place,
Are now gone
And we will never know who they could have become,
Leaving those that loved them behind, wondering-
Why them?
Or why not me?

The silence after the horror sets in
And it turns to sorrow
For you then begin to realize so many innocent lives have been lost,
And the fear inside you grows,
For you do not yet know if it is you that has lost someone that you love.
Even those who don't know anyone,
We grieve every senseless loss with you.

May we all somehow find comfort in each others arms
Strangers and friends,
Let us all come together as fellow human beings
And care about one another,
And help those that are lost by this,
The survivors who live with the sounds and pictures
Of the day that changed their life forever
We have not forgotten any of you,
And remember,
You are not alone in this.

What happened?

Why did it start and why is it not stopping?
Let us never forget anyone who has been affected by school violence,
Let us comfort all of them,
And hope this will be the last.

As we say good-bye to those that were lost,
Let us not forget the pure fragility of life
So make friends wherever and whenever you can
Love as much as you can,
For no place seems to be safe anymore,
And we no longer know when our loved one walks out the door
If they will ever be coming back.
So cherish every minute you have with everyone that you love.

May the souls of those lost, find peace
And watch over those left behind,
Give them your strength and guidance to carry on without you,
And may those who have ever lost, witnessed
Or somehow been involved in such senseless violence,
Somehow, someday, find a way for their heart to heal
And move on,
For we must not let them win.

The nation mourns with you
Not just for the lives lost, or the survivors that carry the scars
But for the loss of innocence,
The loss of fun,
And feeling safe and carefree,
We can all hope that someday it will return.

But I can't help but wonder-
Will it ever really stop?
Will the kid's today ever know the way it used to be?
And will it ever be that way again?

I had the privilege of taking care of a man who had cancer and was facing death. This man and his family were truly inspiring to me. They let me into their home and their lives at such a difficult time, and they did it with open arms. Every time I walked into their home it was filled with love, laughter and strength. He was a teacher and continued to be one, and I was his student. He always had a lesson to teach me, and he was always the one that made me feel better. And when I was having a bad day, it was him that made my day a little brighter. He never showed fear of what lye ahead, and continued to live each day as fully as he could, for he knew his days were limited. And no matter how much pain he was in, he always greeted me with a smile and a joke. The laughter and love in the home was always there, even towards the end. He is the kind of person I can only hope to be someday. He did not want people mourning for him after he was gone; he wanted them to be celebrating and was even taking drink orders for his service. And he passed away peacefully at home with his wife sitting beside him. At his service there was lots of laughter, some tears, and of course drinks and celebration…just as he wanted. I will never forget the things he taught me, the jokes, his smile, and his amazing family. I will never forget my experience with any of them and they will stay in a special place in my heart forever. The family allowed me to read this at his service, and I thank them, it meant the world to me.

A Special Man

I had the privilege of caring for a very special man
A man whose heart was too big for his body
And a sense of humor that could not be shaken,
His home always welcoming
And filled with laughter,
You would never know by looking in his eyes that he was dying.

He was a special man
Who was more courageous then I ever thought someone could be,
For he kept the hope
Even when there was doubt,
And when he knew the hope was gone
He decided it was time to let go,
And even though he did not know the journey that lye ahead for him,
He was not afraid.

He was a very special man
One to whom I will never forget,
Making my job the best job in the world,
Because I got to meet people like him
People who inspire and teach us about what is important in life
For it was him who made me feel better,
Our visits made my days brighter
And he always made me laugh,
Even though he was the one that was in pain
And facing the unknown.

Even though this special man is no longer physically with us
He went in peace, with his love by his side,
And his soul will carry on through the memories of his life,
Even though his laughter has been silenced,
It will live on in those that knew him,
For he knew he could no longer do everything he wanted to do here,
His soul needed to be set free,
To a place without pain and disease.

It was not easy for those who knew this special man to let him go,
He was loved by so many, touched so many lives
It was not easy for him to let go of those he cared so deeply for

But he knew it was time for him to go,
But he knew that it was not good-bye
For he will continue to watch over those close to him,
And guide them through this difficult time
Until they all meet again.

Even though I did not know you long,
I want to thank you for touching my life
And teaching me about the gift of laughter and courage,
Even in the darkest of situations,
You were smiling and laughing.
I promise to remember you fondly,
To have a drink in your honor
Celebrate the life you lived,
And go on living, laughing, and loving,
Just as you wanted.

May you rest in peace with your son by your side
Good-bye for now
And thanks for the memories.

In memory of Erv and his wonderful family who took such good care of him, loving and laughing until the end, you all taught me so much. Thanks for letting me be part of your wonderful family, and thanks for allowing me to care for him

This is about being there for people. Whether it is as friend, family member, co-worker, acquaintance, or even a stranger. Life is hard and we all need someone that we can go to when things get hard, or to help us celebrate the good times. We have all felt lost at times and very alone not knowing if things will ever get better. But the challenges of life are there for us to learn lessons, to grow stronger, but sometimes we just need an extra hand to hold, or a hug to get us through. I don't believe anyone should go through life alone, never having anyone to go to or share things with. We all need love and to be loved and to know that we are not alone in this. For we have all been there a time or two ourselves, learned from mistakes and that knowledge should be shared and passed on to those going through it the first time. It might just take a simple phone call to let someone know you are thinking of him or her, or a simple hug, an outreached hand. Some of the simplest of things make the biggest impact.

So, let us be kind to one another for we are all in this life together. Some of us struggle more then others; and some of us are stronger then others. But we all love, hurt, feel lost, feel alone, confused, or happy at one time or another. Let us help one another out, reach out your hand and help someone through a rough time, or help them celebrate an important time in their life. For you never know when it will be you that needs someone.

I'll Be There

I'll be there when your world is dark
When you can't seem to find the light
I will guide you
And stay with you,
Until the darkness clears
And there is light once again,
And you can find your own way.

I'll be there
When your heart has been broken
And you don't know why,
All you know is the pain that you feel
I will be there to listen
And to hold you,
For I have been there too.

I'll be there
When life is so confusing
And hard,
And you don't even know which way to go
I will help you find your way
And help you make the right decision
On which way to go,
So you can reach your destiny.

I'll be there
Whenever you need me
For whatever reason,
Or if there is no reason
I will give you the support that you need,
And you can lean on me as long as you need to
Until you can stand on your own again.

I'll be there
When life brings you sorrow
And you find yourself having to say good-bye to someone you love
I'll help in anyway I can,
And even if I don't understand

I'll simply just stand by you
For as long as you need me,
I'll be there.

I'll be there
Through the good times and the bad
And the in between times
I will not let you down,
Even when you feel you don't need me
I'll still be behind you
Just in case you need my hand,
All you need to do is reach back and take it.

This is about something that everyone out there has gone through a time or two in their life. It is heartbreak. Everyone has experienced the relationship that, in your eyes, was going just great, you really felt like this could be "the one". Then, you turn around one day and that person is gone. The person who told you everything you wanted to hear, held you so close, kissed you so gently, did everything right, except for stay. Of course, at first you are shocked and confused because there were no signs of them leaving, no argument the night before, there was nothing. And that is what makes this situation so painful and difficult to get over. You have no closure, no explanations, nothing except a big hole in your life and heart where that person once was. It is so hard to pick yourself off of the floor and move on, but know that you are not alone in this, because everyone has had this happen to them at some point in their life. And we have all survived, so will you.

Good-Bye

How do you say good-bye when you are not ready
When your heart is hanging on so tight,
To some kind of hope
Hope that is no longer there.

How does your heart ever heal
When it is so broken,
And lost,
When the person that can make it better
Is the one that is no longer there.

How do you remain strong
And hold your head up
When you feel so weak,
How do you go on
When you feel so lost,
And don't know which way to go.

How do you say good-bye
When your heart doesn't want to
And the tears don't ever seem to stop
You feel so empty inside,
And the pain so deep.

How do you say good-bye
When you never saw it coming
When you thought they would always be there,
But now they are gone forever
And you have to find the strength somehow,
To go on without them.

So many memories made
Thinking you had time to make more memories with them,
You mind always flooded with images of them
Or things that they said,
And each time you close your eyes you see them,
Then your heart aches
Because you realize that is the only place they can ever be now,
Is in your dreams.

How do you say good-bye
When you don't understand why they were taken away
And you long so much just to hear their voice one more time,
You long for their touch,
Just one more time
Because nothing seems to ease the pain.

How do you ever really say good-bye
To someone that has touched your life
Your heart,
Your soul,
To say good-bye to someone that you thought you were going to love
forever?

This poem was inspired by my brother and sister-in-law. I wrote it for their wedding day to represent the love and commitment I have seen between them for ten years. It is about loving someone for who they are, and celebrating each other's dreams. It is about embracing the differences with the one that you love and enjoying those things you have in common. Commitment is about sticking together, being there for one another and taking the good times with the bad. To spend the rest of your life with someone that you love and who loves you, right by your side. Always being grateful for having found that someone and never taking love for granted. For love is what life is really all about, it is the only thing that is real, and the only thing we take with us.

My Wish For You

As you stand together tonight
Under the winter sky,
With the snow beneath your feet
And those who love you all around,
May your heart always be filled with the warmth
And love for one another.

And as you travel down this road called life
Remember there are lesson's a head of you
Some will be unclear,
And difficult to understand
Others will be happy
And some will be painful,
But through it all
May you always find comfort, support,
And love in each other's arms.

May there be lots of happiness
And laughter to celebrate together
Remember to support and respect each other's dreams,
Stand beside one another
And watch them come true
For our destinies are never off course.

Even in the darkest of times
We are learning,
So hold each other a little tighter
Love each other a little more,
And have the comfort of knowing
That you don't have to go through anything alone
For you have each other,
Now and for always.

Remember to wake up every morning
And be thankful for your love,
Because love is the only thing that is real
And the only thing we take with us.
So hold each other tight
Don't walk away,
And never let go,

But if you find that one of you has slipped behind
Stop and reach back for them
Letting them know you are there,
And always will be
For you shall never walk alone again
You shall always walk side-by-side down the journey of life.

May you always love each other with everything you have
And never be afraid to say, "I'm sorry"
Don't ever take your love for granted,
For life is not about how many breaths you take
But how many moments take your breath away,
And I hope your life is filled with many moments that take your
breath away.

This poem came about shortly after a high school classmate/friend committed suicide. It is about the emotions and shock of suddenly losing someone and not knowing why. Knowing in some way that she was in pain and did not reach out for help. Regretting not keeping in touch after high school, but still considering her a friend. It is also about all the other classmates/friends that have died during and after high school. Growing up in a small mountain town, everyone respected one another; you knew them, even if you weren't close friends. And when someone died, you felt the pain, and the loss of them.

To experience so many losses to death at such a young age, there was only one way we all made it through, and that was each other. Our friendships grew stronger; we made new friendships, strengthen old ones, and held each other tight. With each death, we always made our way back to each other, dropping our lives to reunite and support each other. It is a strong and unspoken bond between everyone that will always be there. Like we are always going to be there for each other, no matter what life brings, we know we can get through it because will have each other.

Rain

As the rain falls, running down the windows
Like tears running down your cheeks
Trying to imagine how many tears you must have cried,
Not knowing what your life was like,
How much pain you must have had inside of you
How your heart must have ached just to have someone hold you,
And how dark your world had become
To make you believe there was no way out.

It's hard to imagine you without a big smile on your face
Laughing,
And having lots of friends surrounding you with love,
That is the way we choose to remember you
Because to us—
That was who you truly were,
A person that loved life
And had a big heart full of love to give.

None of us will ever know what changed in you
What pain was in your life,
Or the darkness in your heart and mind,
For we all grew up and life took us our separate ways
Never imagining we would all be back together to say good-bye to
you,
For your life to end in such a violent and tragic way,
With so many unanswered questions, which will always remain with
us.

Even though we didn't stay close
Or keep in touch like we should have,
You were always our friend,
And we all thought about you from time to time
Remembering that big bright smile of yours.

Rain continuing to fall down the car window
Like the tears running down our cheeks
For none of us had to say anything,
Because we all knew that this ride was the ride we had to take
To say our final good-bye to you,
Knowing our lives will not be the same after today.

We have been down this road before

Having to say good-bye to too many friends,
But we all made it through because we held on to one another
So we must, once again, hold each other tight
Knowing what lies ahead,
But also knowing we are going to make it through
Because we have each other,
And always will.

As we say good-bye
Wiping each other's tears away
We will miss you,
But the real you will not be forgotten,
We hope that your pain is over
And the dark and scary days are gone,
You are at peace now
And can once again smile that beautiful smile we remember.

And as we always do,
We stood together at the end of the road to say good-bye
Knowing we must somehow turn around and carry on with our lives,
For it is not our time for our road to end,
But it was yours,
We hope that you are together again
With all our other friends we have lost along the way
Together again, just like old times,
May there be lots of laughter and love,
And peace.

May all of you watch over us
As we turn and walk back down the road of life,
And give us strength to make it through the hard days,
When we miss all of you so much
And guide us as we continue on with our lives,
Reminding us just how fragile life is—
And to stay close to each other, and never let go,
Never let go.

**Dedicated to all of those that Middle Park High School has lost
through the years. None of you have been forgotten, may you all
rest in peace!!**

Sometimes we meet someone and we never think that we could fall in love with them. But then it happens as much as we sometimes fight it, you cannot fight or chose who you love. Even then, sometimes the love is not equal, one person loves more then the other and fights with everything they have to somehow keep that person in our lives, hoping that someday they will learn to love us. It might be that it is because they love us so much that they pull away. They let their fear win over love, so if you feel that someone loves you they probably do, but that doesn't mean they have the strength or ability to actually love you back, if only in their hearts. But because of fear or believing that they don't deserve happiness and love in their life, sometimes we have to let them go. And as painful as that is, we cannot hold on to someone who does not want to be held. We cannot keep someone who does not see the same future we do, or cannot over come their fear. All we can do is hope that someday their heart finds some sort of peace and maybe finds love not with you but with someone else. Because when you truly love someone, you are willing to set them free and all you want for them is happiness and love, and is much as it hurts, you are willing to let them find that with someone else. You are willing to do anything for their happiness, even if that means letting them go even though you want to hold on to them forever.

Love is....

Love is...
Lying next to you without either of us saying a word
Just feeling that I am safe with you next to me,
And feeling the love that is between us
Love that is unspoken,
For it comes from the soul.

Love is...
When my heart fills up every time I think of you
It doesn't matter if we just said good-bye
Or we haven't seen each other in awhile,
I always feel lit up inside with love for you
And I can feel the love you have for me.

Love is....
Looking into your beautiful eyes and seeing how much you care
And every time you touch me
It is like the first time all over again
I never knew what love was before I met you,
But now I know how love feels
And what love is,
Love is you.

Love is....
Always wanting to be with you
Never getting tired of being with you,
Wanting to talk and find out more about you all the time
And finding it so hard to leave your side
Because I always want to be with you,
For being by your side is where I belong
Because being in your arms is home for me,
For I know I will always be safe, protected, and loved there.

Love is....
Taking each other for whom we really are
Excepting each other's faults and celebrating our similarities,
Feeling comfortable about being ourselves around one another,
Having no need to impress
For you are loved for you,

And I know that you love me for me.

Love is…
Being there for each other through the good times and the bad
Laughing and celebrating life together
And being thankful for our love,
Never letting go of each other's hands
And as we grow old together,
Our love will grow too
Stronger then we ever imagined.

Love is….
Somehow finding the strength through my tears
And the pain in my heart
To let you go,
For my love alone is not enough to keep you here,
Or to keep us together,
I cannot keep you where you do not want to be
So I have to love you enough to set you free,
And hopefully someday you will realize that what we had was love,
And that you do deserve to have that in your life,
But I can't make you realize that,
My love is just not that strong alone.

Love is…
Following your heart
And not letting fear lead you through life,
I know you are scared,
I just hope that someday you will really listen to your heart
Listen to what your soul needs,
And that is love.
You can have it all,
If you choose to.
I just hope someday you will wake up missing me
And find your way back,
So I can love you forever.

This poem is about growing up. Inspired by a friend and her little girl. I would just sit back and watch them interact together, and her growing up so fast. In my mind, wondering what she is going to be like as a teenager, and then as an adult. And not just her, but all my friend's kids. Some of them teenagers already. Everyone growing so fast, feeling like it was just yesterday that they were all born. Life does move pretty fast, so it is those little moments, like their first steps that you have to grab on to and treasure, for you cannot go back.

Who You Are Going To Be

As your tiny hand wraps around my finger
I look down at you as you take your first cautious steps
And I wonder who you are going to be.

Your smile lights me up inside
And hearing you laugh brings me joy
I have never known such happiness before you,
And I wonder who you are going to be.

As you grow
And with each accomplishment
I look at you with such pride,
And wonder who you are going to be.

I realize I must let you make your mistakes
And learn your lessons,
Love you with my whole heart
And let you know I will always be there for you,
And I wonder who you are going to be.

Now as we sit and talk
Holding hands,
I realize,
Your hand is no longer little
And neither are you.
You have grown into a beautiful woman,
And it is then that I realized whom you turned out to be.

You turned out to be everything I dreamed you could be
A loving, caring, intelligent, happy person
Who has learned from her lessons
And grown from them,
And is making it in this world just fine.

Even though you are grown
A part of you will always be my little girl,
With her hand wrapped around my finger so tightly,
But I no longer have to wonder who you are going to be.

Inspired by my friend Jody and her daughter, Bea.

About the author:

ERIN MCGRAW is a registered nurse who lives in Denver, Colorado. She grew up in the small ski town of Winter Park, Colorado. She earned her Bachelor's of Science degree in Nursing at Regis University in Denver and has been a nurse for ten years. She already has one book published, entitled "The Journey of the Terminally Ill- Through the Eyes and Heart of a Hospice Nurse". Which encounters her journey and the journey of her patients as they travel down the difficult road of facing a terminal illness. It is available at barnesandnoble.com and amazon.com. She plans to continue to write and her next project is to write a children's book about Guardian Angels.

If you wish to contact her for questions, comments, feedback about this book or her other book, you can contact her at elmrn@msn.com

www.ingramcontent.com/pod-product-compliance
Lightning Source LLC
Chambersburg PA
CBHW020512100426
42813CB00030B/3218/J